In · Time · of · Need

Floods

by Sean Connolly

FRANKLIN WATTS
LONDON·SYDNEY

An Appleseed Editions book

First published in 2004 by Franklin Watts
96 Leonard Street, London, EC2A 4XD

Franklin Watts Australia
45–51 Huntley Street, Alexandria, NSW 2015

© 2004 Appleseed Editions

Created by Appleseed Editions Ltd,
Well House, Friars Hill, Guestling, East Sussex, TN35 4ET

Designed by Ian Butterworth

ISBN 0 7496 5708 1

A CIP catalogue for this book is available from the British Library.

Photographs by:
AP/Wide World Photos, Corbis (AFP, Bettmann, CHINA
FEATURES/CORBIS SYGMA, THOMAS DALLAL/CORBIS SYGMA,
Michael Freeman, London Aerial Photo Library, Sally A. Morgan;
Ecoscene, Bruce Peebles, Reuters, H. David Seawell, Grant Smith,
ST LOUIS POST/CORBIS SYGMA, Stocktrek, YEE EVAN/CORBIS
SYGMA)

Printed in the USA

Contents

WATER OVER ROAD

What Causes Floods?

Many of us have complained when a pipe has broken and the bathroom or kitchen has flooded. Even a small amount of spilled water creates a mess that is hard to clean up. But imagine a flood big enough to soak the entire house, or even sweep it away. That is the sort of flood that millions of people around the world experience each year. And it is not just houses and property that are lost. Some of the deadliest floods in history have killed nearly a million people.

Natural Events

Although floods can become disasters, most of them are part of a natural pattern that scientists call the water cycle. Water moves from clouds to the soil as rain or snow. From

Above: When an area's watershed becomes saturated or blocked, devastating floods can result. Left: Floods can happen so suddenly that people have no time to flee.

the soil, it flows to streams and rivers, and finally to the ocean. Water in the ocean **evaporates**, returning to the clouds to start the cycle again. Most floods take place when the system becomes overloaded.

Water from rain and melting snow flows down from high ground onto an area of land called a **watershed**. The watershed soaks up some of the water, just as a sponge soaks up spilt water. The rest flows into streams that lead to rivers – and then to the sea or a lake. In a way, the watershed is like a giant gutter – sometimes as large as a small country – that drains water safely. If, for some reason, the watershed cannot drain the water fast enough, a flood develops.

Types of Blockage

The Bible tells of a terrible flood that developed after 40 days and 40 nights of rain. In most cases, however, it takes far less time to create a flood. After just a few days of heavy rain, the soil in many areas cannot soak up any more water, and the streams and brooks running off the watershed become too full to drain the extra water. The water flows over their banks and over the banks of the rivers downstream. The level of the floodwater keeps on rising until the rains stop or people find a way of draining off some of the water.

Floods caused by melting snow can be even more dangerous. The problem develops when snow melts while the ground is still frozen. Frozen ground is unable to absorb water. Melting snow has nowhere to go, so it builds up on the surface. Then it begins to flow downhill, causing a dangerous, fast-flowing flood. Such floods develop very quickly, giving people little warning.

People can also cause floods, sometimes without even knowing it. Buildings, car parks and roads can make it harder for the ground in a watershed to soak up water. With nowhere to drain, the floodwaters rise even higher.

Above: A 19th century engraving depicting the great Biblical flood.

In 1989, the destructive power of a flash flood collapsed this railway track in Scotland.

Flash Floods

Some floods, known as **flash floods**, affect a smaller area but can develop far more suddenly. They happen when heavy rains cause small rivers or streams to rise suddenly and overflow. Flash floods can occur with little or no warning. A peaceful stream can suddenly turn into a deadly river. These floods move at incredible speeds and are very powerful. A sudden flash flood can carry away trees, houses, bridges, and almost anything else in its path – including people. The flash flood of the Big Thompson River in Colorado in 1976 caused 139 **casualties** as it swept through homes in a narrow **canyon**.

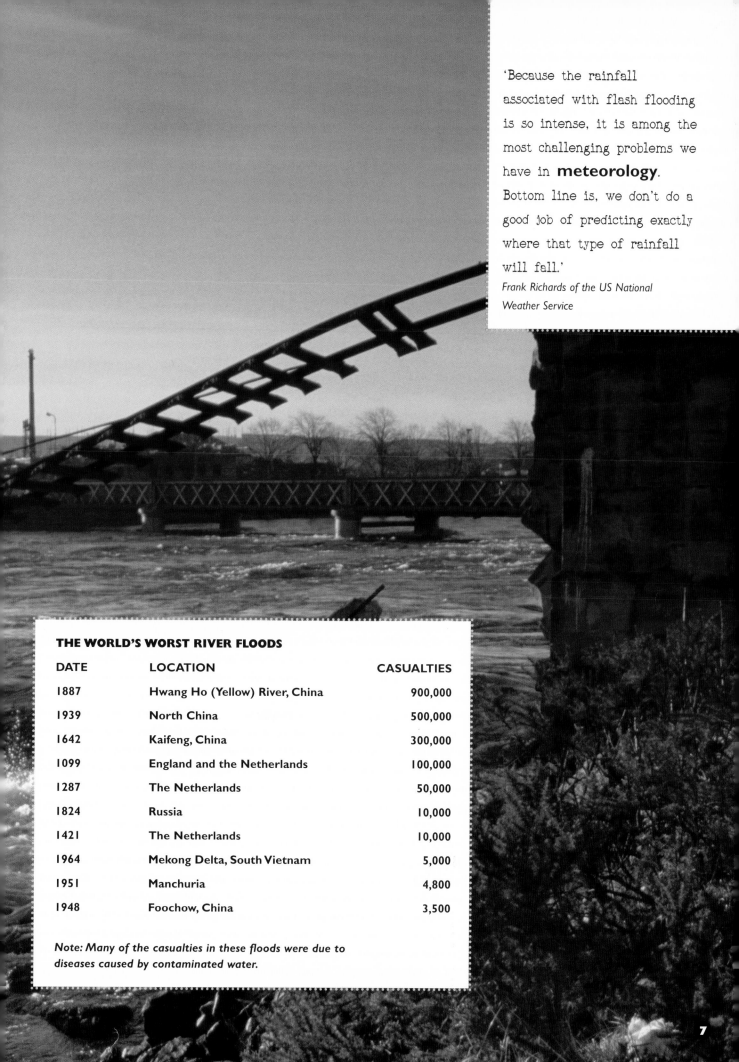

'Because the rainfall associated with flash flooding is so intense, it is among the most challenging problems we have in **meteorology**. Bottom line is, we don't do a good job of predicting exactly where that type of rainfall will fall.'
Frank Richards of the US National Weather Service

THE WORLD'S WORST RIVER FLOODS

DATE	LOCATION	CASUALTIES
1887	Hwang Ho (Yellow) River, China	900,000
1939	North China	500,000
1642	Kaifeng, China	300,000
1099	England and the Netherlands	100,000
1287	The Netherlands	50,000
1824	Russia	10,000
1421	The Netherlands	10,000
1964	Mekong Delta, South Vietnam	5,000
1951	Manchuria	4,800
1948	Foochow, China	3,500

Note: Many of the casualties in these floods were due to diseases caused by contaminated water.

Coastal Chaos

Not all floods are caused by overflowing rivers. Many of the most damaging floods occur when rapidly rising levels of seawater (or even lake water) surge on to low-lying coastal land. Like river floods, coastal floods are very powerful. Many houses, schools and other buildings suffer because of the water itself, which ruins floors and walls, as well as electrical systems and furniture. Other buildings are simply toppled by the force of the water that rushes against them.

Above and left: High tides often create dangerous waves that can lead to coastal flooding.

Below: The heavy rains and high tides that often accompany hurricanes can devastate coastal areas.

Many coastal floods develop when there is a combination of a full or new moon and a **high tide**. This combination causes seawater to rise much higher than normal – and if there is a strong wind blowing in from the ocean, the water rises even higher. A particularly high tide, which is normally linked to a severe storm such as a hurricane, is called a **surge**. As a hurricane approaches the coast, its winds force water towards the shore. When the edge of the storm reaches the shallow waters of the coast, the water piles up. Winds of hurricane strength force the water onto the shore. Waves pound the coast as tonnes of moving water hammer away at any structure built on the coastline. In 1970, a hurricane in the Bay of Bengal in the Indian Ocean caused the greatest sea flood disaster in history, killing 266,000 people.

Killer Waves

Some terrible coastal floods are caused by a single wave, known as a **tsunami**. Some people call these 'tidal waves', but they have nothing to do with tides. Instead, they are caused by underwater earthquakes and volcanoes. Tsunamis build up enormous speed – up to 805 kilometres per hour – and can rise to more than 25 metres by the time they reach land. In 1964, a tsunami struck the Kodiak Island and southern coast of Alaska soon after an earthquake hit Anchorage.

'I came home on Friday, April 18, from two hours of **sandbagging** wondering how anyone could do that for so long. I was dirty, sweaty, and sore from my legs up. People were determined to save their homes. We didn't have school that day. You couldn't flip a channel on TV without seeing the news of the flood.'

Sara, a 13 year-old from North Dakota in America, describing how people prepared for the flood in 1997

Warning
Signs

Many countries have national weather centres to keep track of dangerous weather. Their job is to give people warning before these conditions develop and advise on what to do when they occur. The terms on the opposite page are used in America to give weather alerts on television and radio stations when floods seem likely.

Above: A meteorologist tracks storms by watching satellite images at the Observatory Meteorological Centre in Hong Kong.

Flood watch: A high flow or overflow of water from a river is possible. The flood watch can also apply to heavy drainage of water into low-lying areas. These watches are generally issued for flooding that is expected to occur at least six hours after heavy rains have ended.

Flood warning: Flooding is actually occurring or is about to take place in the warning area.

Flash flood watch: Flash flooding is possible in the watch area. Flash flood watches generally refer to flooding that is expected to occur within six hours after heavy rains have ended.

Flash flood warning: Flash flooding is actually occurring or is about to take place in the warning area. Flash flood warnings may be issued as a result of torrential rains, a dam failure, or ice jamming the flow of rivers.

Coastal flood watch: Land along the coast could become flooded within 12 to 36 hours.

Coastal flood warning: Land along the coast is expected to become, or has become, flooded by seawater.

Danger
Unleashed

Whether it builds up over days and weeks or suddenly erupts after a heavy storm, a flood is frightening evidence of nature's force. The power of water – not simply to soak things, but also to carry them away – takes many people by surprise. When a flood threatens, many people living in high-risk areas manage to secure valuable goods on higher ground. If the flood warnings are urgent, they leave their homes for safer places.

Other preparations, such as putting sandbags in place on riverbanks and against houses, can prevent some

Above: Sandbags could not stop the rising waters of this river in America in 1993.
Left: When floodwaters rise quickly, they can often catch people off-guard.

damage. Still, it is usually dangerous to remain behind during a flood. This is obvious to anyone who has seen pictures of houses swept away by a flash flood or battered by waves in a coastal storm. It is also true of floods in which the water level rises gradually. Houses, factories and warehouses can collapse because of damage from standing water. Bridges become unsafe to cross. Wells become **contaminated** when materials carried by floodwater seep into the water supply. Unsafe drinking water can cause a range of serious diseases. It can be especially dangerous in poorer countries where medicine is in short supply.

Below: Floodwaters can leave behind material and debris that contaminate drinking water and make homes unsafe.

THE FLOOD OF THE CENTURY

The Mississippi is the longest river in North America. It is often considered part of a larger river system, the Mississippi-Missouri. Together, they make up the third-longest river in the world, carrying water more than 6,000 kilometres. This water helps to irrigate much of the best farmland in the Midwestern United States. But the Mississippi can also cause terrible damage when it floods.

Some of the worst Mississippi floods took place in 1993. By late spring, the region had been hit with almost constant rain. More than 20 centimetres of rain fell on North and South Dakota, Wisconsin and Minnesota on June 10 alone. Exactly a month later, the weather station at Fort Madison, Iowa, reported that it had rained for 54 of the previous 58 days. More than 100 rivers leading into the Mississippi – and the great river itself – had begun to flood. Bridges connecting cities and states were closed, dams burst, farms were SUBMERGED and property was swept away. By mid-July, the Mississippi had spread more than 11 kilometres beyond its normal banks.

About 41,500 square kilometres of farmland – an area twice the size of Wales – were underwater when the floods were at their worst at the end of July. Nine states were affected. More than 26 million sandbags were used to try to protect property. The rains finally stopped in August, and river levels began to fall. But the flood had already done its terrible damage: 52 people died and more than $12 billion in property was damaged. It soon became known as 'the flood of the century'.

When rivers burst their banks, floodwaters can consume large areas of farmland – ruining crops and damaging homes and roads.

'Our stomachs dropped as we stumbled across the trailer park that had been completely **annihilated** by the excessive rain and mud. Homes were overturned and in shambles, and we shuddered to think about what the determined rescue crews would find.'

Mandy Striegl, a college student, describing a flash flood in 1997 in Colorado

UNEXPECTED TRAGEDY

Heavy rain and strong GALES in November 2001 caused a series of flash floods in Algeria, Africa's second largest country. One of the worst affected areas was the capital, Algiers, where dozens of people were killed and more than 2,000 families lost their homes. Many residents said that the disaster could have been avoided if the Algerian government had not sealed underground sewers running through the city in 1998. Algeria's rulers were trying to stop anti-government rebels from using the underground tunnels as hiding places. 'These tunnels could have channelled away a large amount of water and avoided the CATASTROPHE,' said resident Mustapha Dajaballah. Water from heavy rains was not drawn off through sewage pipes and instead rushed down the roads, sweeping away everything in its path.

During the 1993 flood, the flow of water in the swollen Mississippi River in America, would have filled Wembly Stadium in about one minute.

Scene of the
Rescue

Nature can surprise people at any time, dumping rain for weeks in a region that is normally dry, or unleashing a coastal storm that keeps changing its course as it heads toward land. Even countries that are accustomed to floods can be taken by surprise by the force of a flood. The extent of a flood – and its suddenness – call for a quick reaction on the part of rescue workers.

Above: Flood victims often rely on international assistance to get much-needed food and medical supplies. Left: The top priority for rescue workers is quickly getting people out of harm's way.

Rescue Operations

The most important job in any emergency is to get people to safety and to make sure that those who are injured or sick receive medical treatment. Other natural disasters, such as earthquakes and fires, block off roads and train lines, but rescuers can usually reach the disaster scene by air or in four-wheel drive trucks. A flood is different. In addition to blocking road and train connections, it covers much of the surrounding land with dangerous, unpredictable, flowing water. There are few dry places large enough to land a rescue plane, and heavy rains make it difficult for helicopters to fly. Often the only way to reach flood victims is by boat. Flat-bottomed boats and rafts make their way through flooded villages. It is a long and dangerous process, since whirling currents and hidden trees can turn the rescuers into victims in an instant.

Below: In Bangladesh, two women use a raft to keep their food supplies dry during severe flooding in 2000.

Above: Many flood victims forced from their homes need emergency shelter, especially during prolonged periods of flooding.

The Long Haul

Another difficulty for rescue operations is how long floods can last. Rescuers can arrive at the scene of an earthquake or tornado the day after it hits. They know that nature has done its damage and the rescue can begin. A flood, on the other hand, can last for months. Some people need to be rescued immediately, while other victims choose to stay behind to protect their houses and farms. The people who are rescued need emergency shelter, and the people who stayed behind may need help and supplies.

During the Vietnam flood of late 2000, rescuers travelled through the affected regions with medicine, extra boats and fishing equipment. With this help, families could look after themselves without draining the limited amount of emergency supplies. As one villager, Tran Thi Cuc, put it: 'We cannot rely on handouts. None of the assistance provided is **sustainable**. This is why we need boats and fishing gear – so that we may find our own food and sustain ourselves for months.'

After a flood in Cambodia in 2000 affected nearly two million people, relief workers called for 13,600 tonnes of food to meet immediate aid needs.

HELP IN THE AIR

The terrible floods that hit Mozambique and other southern African countries in early 2000 made it hard for rescuers to reach the worst-hit areas. It was hard to know which roads were still able to support cars and trucks. The US Air Force sent seven cargo planes to the region. Six of the planes dropped relief equipment for the victims in areas that still had enough dry ground to act as landing fields. The seventh plane had a different job. It flew all over the flooded region, making video images of which roads were still open and which areas were affected most by the flood. This information helped rescue organisers to send food and medicine to the hardest-hit places safely and efficiently.

'When the floods came, I managed to get to a tall tree which I climbed. I stayed there until Tuesday, so I was three days in the tree. I was very tired but I had to stay awake. One night I fell asleep by accident and I fell down into the water. But I couldn't climb back up because I was too tired, so I stayed in the water until the next evening.'
Helena Vuma describing her wait for relief after Mozambique's floods in 2000

'We still face starvation. The rice and other material aid that was given to us only lasted for a few days, and then we go for stretches without food. There were times when we were so desperate we sought water hyacinths to eat at the risk of drowning.'
Madame Nguyen Thi Nhan of Tan Lap, Vietnam, describing life after the December 2000 flood

'Nobody reached our village for help. People are dying of snake bites. Women and children in our village are still waiting for food. The government is doing nothing.'
Flood survivor Biswanath Mandal after the floods that hit eastern India in 2000

Left: Victims of Mozambique's 2000 floods are airlifted aboard a South African helicopter and brought to safety.

Counting the Cost

It is hard to put an exact price on the amount of damage caused by a large flood. The worst cost, of course, is the loss of human life. Thousands of people can drown, be swept away or crushed, or face starvation because of a flood. An even greater number of people lose their homes and everything they own – as well as the chance to plant or harvest the crops they need to survive. Some of these costs continue for years after a flood, as the victims struggle to rebuild their lives.

A flood in a wealthy place such as the United States or western Europe can affect the lives of thousands of people. After the Mississippi River flood in 1993, more than 31,800 square kilometres of good farmland were made

Above and left: Floods can cause millions of pounds worth damage to homes, businesses, and vehicles.

useless. Thousands of people lost their jobs and houses, and many families are still struggling to make a living. For flood victims in poorer countries, the results can be much worse. Their governments have less money to help them, and often they must look after themselves as best they can.

Coping with Disease

In addition to facing the destruction of their houses and property, flood victims in poorer countries run the risk of becoming very sick from a range of diseases. Some of the illnesses can be traced to not having enough food, but most are caused by drinking dirty water. Relief workers distribute **purification** tablets, which people can dissolve in their drinking water to get rid of possible contamination.

Without such tablets, flood victims would be forced to boil water in order to make it safe to drink. But floods carry away pots and pans that could be used for boiling. Worse still, it is almost impossible to find enough dry wood to build a fire to heat the water.

Above: Bengali flood victims.

During the flood in Bangladesh in 2000, nearly two-thirds of the country lay underwater after three months of heavy rains. The flood was the country's worst in more than a century.

Below: Recovering from floods can be more difficult for people living in poorer nations.

'Gardens were destroyed. Basements with school books gone. Mud was everywhere. In the countryside and small villages, livestock was drowned or slaughtered. With nothing to eat, when a pig would swim by, it was often only a few moments before it became lunch. Farmers no longer have the animals that were once their source of income.'

Woody Renn, a volunteer who witnessed the 2002 floods in the Czech Republic

'I am 70 years old. In all my life, I have not seen floods worse than what we are experiencing. I have lived through a series of wars. Fleeing from these wars was easier than fleeing from this flood.'

Nguyen Thi Nginh, describing floods along the Mekong River, Vietnam, in 2000

Living with Floods

While most people think of only the hardships caused by floods, farmers in some countries expect and even rely on floods to earn a living. Floodwaters usually carry rich soil that stays behind on farmland once the waters have fallen back. For thousands of years, Egyptian farmers have depended on this river-carried soil, known as **silt**, to improve their farms when the Nile floods each year.

Farmers in the Asian country of Bangladesh have also come to rely on silt from three great rivers – the Ganges, the Brahmaputra and the Meghna. Their country is a low-lying **flood plain** for these rivers. Sometimes, however, the welcome floods of Bangladesh turn into a nightmare. During a flood in 2000, some villages in Bangladesh were buried under 3 metres of silt. Roads and buildings were swept away in more than half the country, leaving more than 20 million people without homes.

Right: People in Bangladesh rely on floods to improve the fertility of farmland, but the severe flooding in 2000 left millions without homes.

'I've been here for nearly two weeks, but I have eaten only twice in that time. I've also heard from other people arriving from my village that when the water had gone down my house was broken into and everything was stolen – my cooking pots, blankets, everything.'
Julietta Maundla, speaking at a flood relief camp after Mozambique's 2000 floods

'Day after day we stayed inside using the raft for cooking and other purposes. The raft was also our only hope for survival if the house gave in to the current or the [silt] deposit level rose further.'
Abdul Karim, who lived on a raft for weeks after floods buried his village in Bangladesh in 2000

Left: Even people who are used to living with floods are often not prepared for the many problems floods can cause.

The World Reacts

As World War II ended in 1945, world leaders founded the United Nations (UN) as a way for countries to come together to discuss peace. But the role of the UN soon expanded as it tried to deal with other problems such as hunger, health and natural disasters. The UN is now the most important international group for organising emergency relief. Governments in countries facing disasters such as floods usually turn to the United Nations first for help.

The UN has many departments that provide emergency relief and care for the thousands of people who lose their homes during a flood or other crisis. It often works alongside the International Red Cross, an organisation that specialises in helping the sick and wounded in times of war and natural disaster. Together, they make sure that the

Above: When developing countries are devastated by floods, other nations often come to their aid by providing food and medical supplies.

world hears about disasters as they happen, and encourage individual countries to provide help. Groups that concentrate on particular aspects of relief, such as the International Rescue Corps (IRC), plan their missions with advice from the United Nations.

Changing Roles

Other relief organisations are committed to providing a range of ongoing help to **developing countries**. Many of these international organisations are prepared to take on new and changing responsibilities during a disaster. Organisations such as Oxfam, CARE, World Vision, and Save the Children have people working in many developing countries all the time. Their role is to help the countries produce enough food for the future and create more opportunities for education and good medical treatment. In an emergency such as a flood, these organizations help provide emergency relief. Their knowledge of the local area and the partnerships they have built up with local people are very valuable for the relief effort.

'As news of the flood in the Mekong delta trickled into Boston, I imagined images of people suffering from flood, **famine** and misfortune. But I could never have imagined the depth of suffering I encountered as an eyewitness to the tragedy unfolding in the Mekong delta.'
Ngan Nguyen of Oxfam speaking of Vietnam's flood in 2000

Below: International and government aid can save lives when floodwaters get out of control. Here, a South African Defence Force helicopter rescues flood victims from a rooftop in northern Mozambique in 2000.

Looking Ahead

Floods are natural events, and there is no chance of ever preventing them entirely. The water cycle, which provides water for all plants and animals, will continue to feed streams and rivers around the world. Heavy rains, melting snows and coastal storms will continue to upset the balance of this cycle, producing floods in low-lying areas. And with cities and towns continuing to expand on land that once acted as a watershed, floods could be more frequent and more damaging in the future.

Nonetheless, with the right amount of study and planning, governments and individuals can get a better idea of where and when to expect floods – and possibly reduce the damage when a flood occurs. Some regions of the world have lived with regular floods for thousands of years, and it takes a very unusual flood to upset their lives. Other places use traditional and modern technology to predict and control floods.

Above: An embankment in Illinois gives way to rushing waters from the Mississippi River in 1993, flooding farmland. Left: Floods are as hard on animals as they are on people.

Traditional Methods

One method of controlling a flood is to stop a river from overflowing its banks. Many regions of the world use **dykes** and **embankments** to do this, raising the banks of a river so that it will be harder to overflow. But these methods do not really solve the problem: they often shift it downstream, where increased water flow will cause even greater damage. If the river does burst over an embankment, the sudden rush of water is even more damaging than the gradual rise of a normal flood.

The best solution to the problem is to build channels and canals to take extra water away from areas at risk for flooding. Such canals help with the natural work of streams and small rivers in a watershed, and they can take water to areas that need it.

Twenty thousand towns in the United States are built on flood plains, but only about 1,000 communities have local flood warning systems.

Below: This canal irrigates an Egyptian field with water from the Nile River and helps alleviate the likelihood of a dangerous flood.

Prediction

Life would be much easier for people living near rivers if they had a clear idea of when to expect floods. The US National Weather Service has become a world leader in predicting floods. It uses a system of 12 river forecast centres to make long-range predictions for 97 percent of the United States. Information from local stations goes to these centres, where scientists make flood forecasts by comparing current conditions with the history of an area. They know what type of weather to expect in each season, the shape of major rivers, and the type of soil on the land near the rivers. All of this information can give a clear picture of whether a severe flood is likely. This information is used to send out flood warnings and alerts.

Cutting-edge technology helps national weather organisations with their work. The first orbiting satellites were launched to help predict weather. Weather scientists have found that satellite information can even help them predict flash floods, which were once considered impossible to predict. Satellites send images of clouds back to Earth each half hour. Scientists study these pictures for changes in cloud growth and watch for changes in temperature – both clues to sudden, flood-producing rainstorms.

Right: Satellite photos are a vital tool in meteorologists' efforts to predict flood-inducing storms. Opposite: Boats are often the only way that victims can safely navigate their flooded villages.

NATURAL PROTECTION

One of the best ways to prevent a flood is to do nothing at all, and let nature work things out for itself. If a river is allowed to spread out naturally onto its flood plain, the flow downstream is slowed. The flood plain can hold huge amounts of water that are held back from the main river. If it is allowed to flood in this way the river creates less damage downstream.

In many areas, however, flood plains have been built upon, and this can prevent water from soaking into the ground.

Glossary

annihilated completely destroyed

canyon a long, narrow valley with steep sides

casualties people killed or injured

catastrophe a terrible disaster

contaminated mixed with materials that are unsafe for eating or drinking

developing countries countries (mainly in Africa, Asia and Latin America) that have few industries and rely on basic farming for their economy

dykes walls built along rivers or other bodies of water as protection against floods

embankment raised ground along a river that acts as a barrier to floodwaters

evaporates changes from a liquid into a gas (as water turns into water vapour)

famine a serious shortage of food over a large area

flash floods destructive floods that develop suddenly in a local area

flood plain a flat area on either side of a river that is underwater during a flood

gales very strong winds, usually part of a severe storm

high tide the highest level that seawater reaches in its twice-daily tide cycle

meteorology the scientific study of weather

purification getting rid of dangerous materials such as chemicals or bacteria

sandbagging using bags of sand to build protective walls against rising floodwater

satellites unmanned spacecrafts that orbit Earth

silt rich soil carried by rivers

submerged completely underwater

surge a very high tide caused by a coastal storm

sustainable able to be supported or maintained for a long period

tsunami a powerful wave caused by an undersea earthquake or volcanic eruption

watershed an area of land that drains into a stream or river

Further Information

Books

DK Guide to the Savage Earth,
   by Trevor Day.
   London: Dorling Kindersley, 2001.

Visual Factfinder: Planet Earth,
   by Neil Curtis and Michael Allaby.
   London: Grisewood and Dempsey, 1993.

The Usborne Book of Weather Facts,
   by Anita Ganeri.
   London: Usborne, 1992.

Web sites

Medicins Sans Frontieres
www.msf.org

International Committee of the Red Cross
and Red Crescent (ICRC)
www.icrc.org

Weather
http://www.eduplace.com/links/gen/weather.html

Disasters
http://www.eduplace.com/links/gen/disasters.html

Index